World of Faiths

Islam

Fatma Amer

QED Publishing

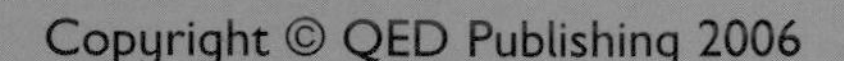

First published in the UK in 2006 by
QED Publishing
A Quarto Group company
226 City Road
London EC1V 2TT
www.qed-publishing.co.uk

Reprinted in 2007

A catalogue record for this book is available from the British Library.

ISBN 978 1 84538 707 5

Written by Fatma Amer
Designed by Tall Tree Books
Editor Louisa Somerville
Consultant John Keast
Illustrations Laure Fournier

Publisher Steve Evans
Creative Director Zeta Davies
Editorial Director Jean Coppendale

Printed and bound in China

Picture credits
Key: t = top, b = bottom, c = centre, l = left, r = right, FC = front cover

Alamy Arkreligion.com 20/ Jochem Wijnands 19tr; **Ark Religion** Tibor Bognar 1/ David Clegg 13tr/ Helen Rogers 5t, 6tl, 7c, 14, 15t&b, 17t, 19b; **Corbis** Ali Haider/epa 21tr/ Ann Johansson 4/ Chris Lisle FC/ Bazuki Muhammad/Reuters 18/ SUPRI/Reuters 23b; **Getty Images** James Emmerson 22/ Abid Katib 9tr; **Trip** 5b, 6br, 7b, 8, 9b, 12, 16, 21bl, 23, 24, 25t, 27t/ Chris Rennie 7t/ Adina Tovy 25b/ Bob Turner 26.

Picture on page 7 (tr) courtesy of Islamic Relief.

Words in **bold** are explained in the glossary on page 30.

Contents

What is a Muslim?

A Muslim is a follower of Islam, the religion based on the teachings of a sacred book called the Qur'an, which Muslims believe contains the word of God. The word Islam means 'peace' and 'submission' in Arabic. All Muslims, wherever they are from, try to live by the teaching of **Allah** (God). They try to make everything in their life perfect, for Allah's sake.

Islam around the world

Muslims believe that the Qur'an was revealed to the **prophet** Muhammad who lived over 1400 years ago, in the country now known as Saudi Arabia. Within fewer than 100 years of his death, Islam had spread far and wide. Today, there are Muslims living around the globe. They are of different nationalities, come from different cultures and speak many different languages.

▼ These Muslim girls are from California, in the United States.

What do Muslims believe?

Muslims believe that there is only one God, Allah, who created humans and the universe for them to live in out of his love. Muslims also believe that Allah chose prophets to show them how to lead their lives in peace and harmony.

▲ The Qur'an is written in **Arabic**. Here, an English translation is on the left-hand side of each page.

◀ These Muslims are praying at the London Central **Mosque**.

'Say (O Muslims), "We believe in Allah and that which has been sent down to us."'
Qur'an 2:136

Prophets

Muslims believe that Allah spoke to the prophets through his angels, who then delivered his message to people. The chain of prophets starts with Adam. It includes Ibrahim (Abraham), Musa (Moses) and Isa (Jesus), and ends with Muhammad.

The five acts of worship

Islam is based on five acts (duties) of worship that Muslims perform. They are also known as the Five Pillars, as if Islam were a strong building held up by five pillars.

▼ Arabic writing of the Shahadah on a tile in the Topkapi Palace in Istanbul, Turkey. It means "There is no other god but God, and Muhammad is the messenger of God."

The first pillar

The first pillar is Shahadah, meaning 'declaration of faith'. The declaration says that Allah is the only God, and that Muhammad was his messenger. This declaration is repeated by all Muslims in their daily prayers.

The second pillar

The second pillar is Salah, meaning 'prayer'. Muslims pray five times a day. Prayer times are at dawn, midday, early afternoon, just after sunset and at night-time. Muslims pray either on their own or in groups. All adult Muslims should attend midday Friday prayers at a mosque.

▶ This boy is praying on a prayer mat called a sajjada.

The third pillar

The third pillar is Zakah, meaning 'giving to the poor and needy'. Every Muslim who can afford it gives at least 2.5 per cent of their yearly earnings to charity. This is to guard against selfishness and greed, and to allow those who are able to share what they have.

▲ These children have received aid from Islamic Relief, a British-based charity.

▼ These Muslim children in London have finished their fast, and are 'breaking' it with a meal.

The fourth pillar

The fourth pillar is Sawm, meaning **fasting**. Muslims do not eat or drink from dawn until sunset during **Ramadan**, the ninth month in the Islamic calendar. This helps Muslims to practise self control. In Muslim countries, during Ramadan evenings, children visit homes in their area chanting rhymes to celebrate the fast.

The fifth pillar

The fifth pillar is Hajj, meaning '**pilgrimage**'. Muslims hope to make the pilgrimage to the holy city of **Makkah** at least once in their lives. Makkah is home to the **Ka'ba**. Muslims believe that the Ka'ba was the first place on Earth built for the purpose of worshipping God.

▲ Thousands of pilgrims praying at the Ka'ba, in Makkah.

Muhammad, the last prophet

Muslims believe that Muhammad was the last and final prophet. Muhammad was born into a noble family in Makkah in 571CE. When he grew up he became a merchant. He was a trustworthy and wise man, and the people of Makkah used to ask for his advice and guidance.

▼ The cave of Hira, the place where the prophet Muhammad used to meditate.

The angel's visit

One day, when he was 40 years old, Muhammad was **meditating** in the cave of Hira, outside Makkah, when he had a vision of the angel Jibril (Gabriel) telling him repeatedly to say the words, "Recite in the name of your Lord, who created man from a clinging substance." The words meant that there was only one god, who was very powerful and had created humans.

More messages

The angel visited the prophet Muhammad many more times to reveal more of Allah's words. Muhammad memorized them and **recited** them to his companions, who memorized them in turn. All the words were recorded in the book that came to be known as the Qur'an.

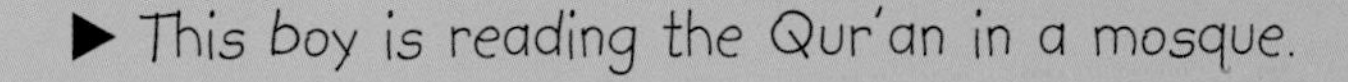

▶ *This boy is reading the Qur'an in a mosque.*

Leaving Makkah

At the time when Muhammad was alive, the people of Makkah worshipped **idols**. They also traded in the idols to make money. They turned against Muhammad, whose new religion they saw as a threat to their way of earning their living as no-one would want to buy idols any longer. As a result, Muhammad and his followers **migrated** to **Madinah**, where Muhammad lived for the rest of his life and built the first mosque.

▲ *Makkah, home of the Ka'ba, is now the most holy Muslim city.*

Muhammad's migration to Madinah

Twelve years had passed since the angel had first visited Muhammad. The number of people becoming Muslim in Makkah grew, but they began to be bullied by some rich merchants, called the Quyrash, who did not like what Muhammad had to say. The merchants were worried that they would lose their powerful position in the city if people began to follow Allah. To prevent this, they stopped people trading or being friends with Muslims.

Allah told Muhammad to ask the Muslims to go from Makkah to the city of Madinah, where they would be welcomed and could live peacefully. It was much to ask, as they would be torn away from their families and would have to leave their homes behind. Muhammad stayed behind until almost everyone had gone. He finally left one night with Abu Bakr, his best friend and most trusted companion.

So that the Quraysh would not immediately suspect Muhammad was leaving, his cousin Ali stayed behind in his bed. The Quraysh were furious when they found out that Muhammad has escaped, and pursued him at once.

Muhammad and his friend Abu Bakr rode through the desert all night, but the next day it was too hot to ride and they hid in a cool cave to rest. In order to protect his prophet, Allah caused a spider to spin its web over the entrance to the cave, and a dove to build her nest and lay eggs nearby.

This threw the Quraysh off the scent as they did not believe that anyone could possibly have entered the cave without destroying the web or scaring the dove away. Muhammad and Abu Bakr were able to continue their journey and were welcomed by everyone when they at last reached Madinah.

The Qur’an

The Qur’an, the sacred book of Islam, is written in the Arabic language. Muslims believe that it contains the exact words of God, told to Muhammad by the angel Jibril. Because the words of the Qur’an were both told to Muhammad and written down in Arabic, Muslims everywhere try to learn Arabic in order to read it. Even now, although the Qur’an was translated into many languages, Muslims must learn how to read (or at least recite) part of the Qur’an in Arabic.

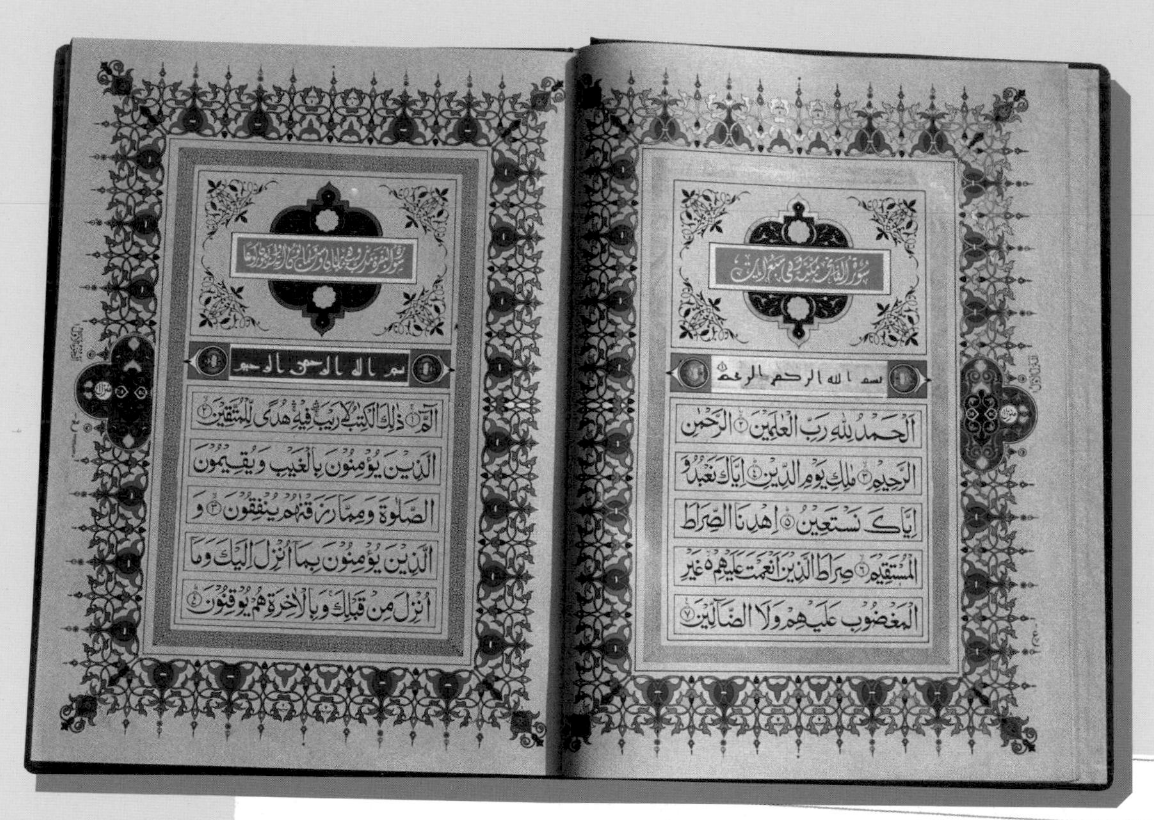

◀ Some copies of the Qur’an are very highly decorated with striking patterns in rich colours.

Calligraphy

The Qur’an is traditionally written using **calligraphy**. Some ancient copies of the Qur’an are displayed in museums around the world. Even now, although printed copies are available, a Qur’an written by hand by a skilled calligrapher is a treasured and precious possession.

Learning the Qur'an

The Qur'an is divided into 30 parts and contains 114 suras (chapters). Each sura is made up of verses that were revealed to Muhammad at different times and in different places. Muslims try to memorize as many suras as possible. A person who learns the whole Qur'an has the honorary title of 'hafiz'. People do their best to make their voices beautiful when they recite the Qur'an. Some people even choose to be professional Qur'an reciters, and recite the Qur'an as their job.

▲ These four boys in Lombok, Indonesia, are learning the Qur'an.

Reciting the Qur'an

In Muslim countries during Ramadan, competitions are held for adults and children to see who can memorize and recite the whole Qur'an, or parts or it. People spend a long time training for such events. Many Muslims also like to start everyday activites by reciting a few verses from the Qur'an to ask for Allah's blessings upon what they intend to do.

Write your name in Arabic

You will need: coloured card • scrap paper • pencil coloured pencils • felt-tip or metallic pens • sequins • glue

1 Find a website that shows the alphabet in both Arabic and English (see page 32). Practise writing your name in Arabic on the scrap paper.

2 Write your name in Arabic, in pencil, on the card. Then go over the letters neatly with a felt-tip or metallic pen. Decorate the card with sequins and geometric designs.

Visiting a mosque

Johnny was very excited because he had arrived in London from Australia to spend a week with Ali, his pen pal. Ali had promised to take Johnny to see all his favourite places in London. "Why don't we go and visit the London Central Mosque?" said Ali. "It's down the road from my house and it's my favourite place!"

On the way, Johnny saw the gold dome of the mosque from a distance. He was curious as he had never seen a mosque before. Ali explained, "Muslims can pray anywhere, provided that the place is clean. However, mosques are our places of worship. We believe that the Ka'ba in Makkah was the first place of worship on Earth. It was built by Adam. We face it when we pray."

▼ The London Central Mosque has a large golden dome.

▲ The main hall has a grand chandelier.

As they entered, Ali pointed out the building's features: "All mosques have at least one **minaret**, a dome and a library. I normally sit in the library once a week after my Arabic and Qur'anic lessons next to the prayer hall." The boys took off their shoes and placed them in the nearby rack before entering the building. The main area inside the mosque is the prayer hall, where worshippers gather during prayer times. The prayer hall is normally carpeted, but has no furniture. Pictures of people or animals are not allowed inside the prayer hall. The niche in the wall facing the worshippers is called the **mihrab**. It shows the direction of Makkah, where the Ka'ba is.

▲ This Imam is giving children sweets for Eid.

A prayer timetable tells the worshippers when each prayer begins and ends. As the two friends heard the call to prayer, Ali pointed out the **Imam**. "Come on Johnny," he said, "Lets go and meet him!" The Imam explained to the boys, "My job is to lead the prayer, so I stand in front of the worshippers." As Johnny watched the people praying, he thought about how much he had learned during his visit to the mosque, and how much his friend Ali had taught him about his religion.

Festivals and celebrations

Festivals and other Muslim celebrations are very colourful and happy occasions, especially for children. People wish each other well and exchange presents and beautiful cards decorated with pictures of mosques or Arabic calligraphy. The word for festival in Arabic is 'Eid', and the most important festivals in Islam are Eid-ul Fitr, at the end of Ramadan, and Eid-ul Adha.

Ramadan

Each day during Ramadan, Muslim families gather at sunset to eat a meal together. They eat after first saying prayers and breaking the fast with dates and milk. All adults fast during Ramadan, and some parents let their children fast for a few hours each day, too. Children who manage to fast for any length of time are normally given special treatment to encourage them. Daily fasting ends with the Festival of Eid-ul Fitr.

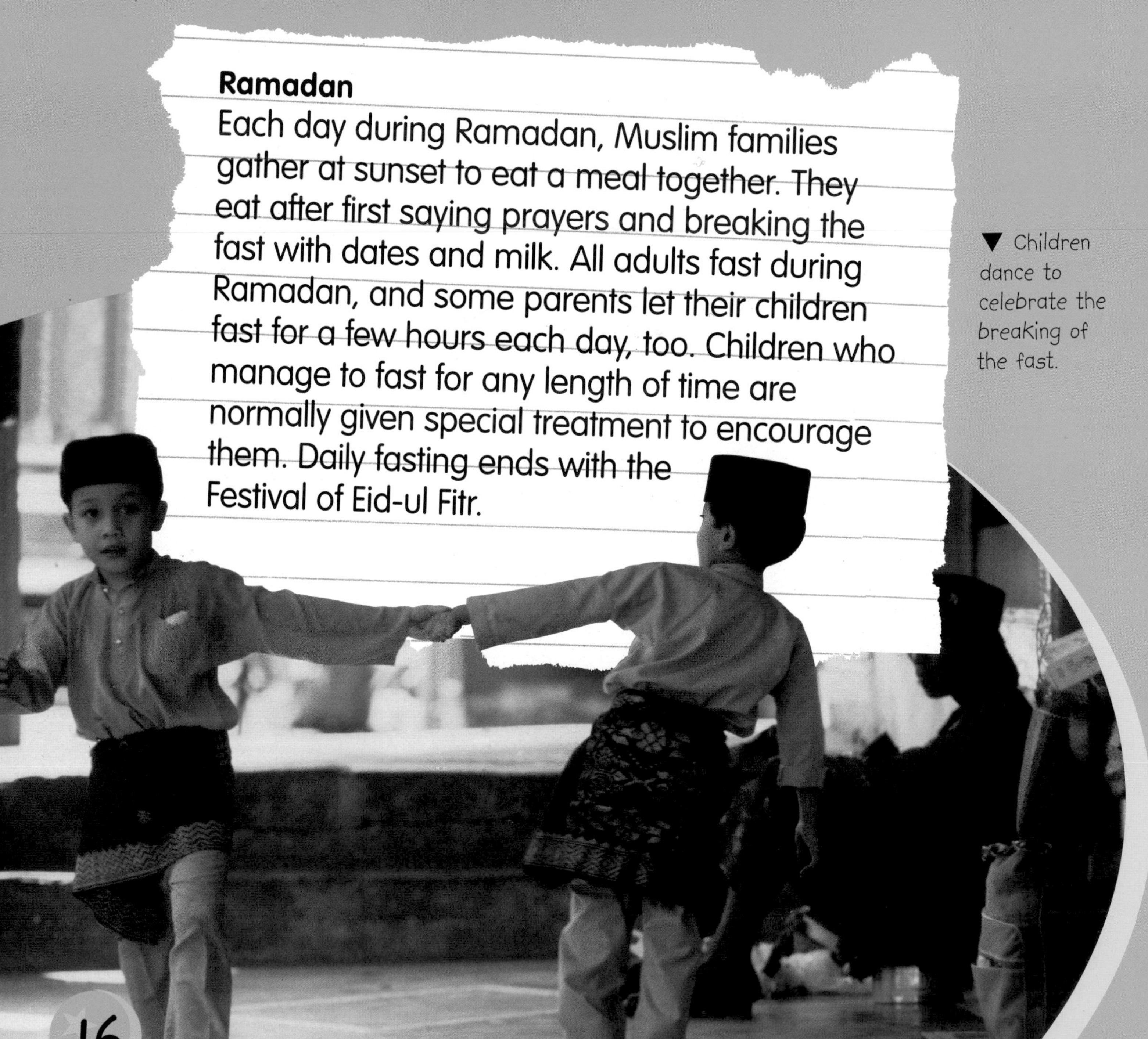

▼ Children dance to celebrate the breaking of the fast.

Breaking the fast

Eid-ul Fitr (festival of breaking the fast) starts at the end of Ramadan. Families gather in the homes of their eldest relative to exchange gifts and prepare special sweet dishes to be shared and eaten together. It is an especially joyful time for the children because they get new clothes and extra pocket money.

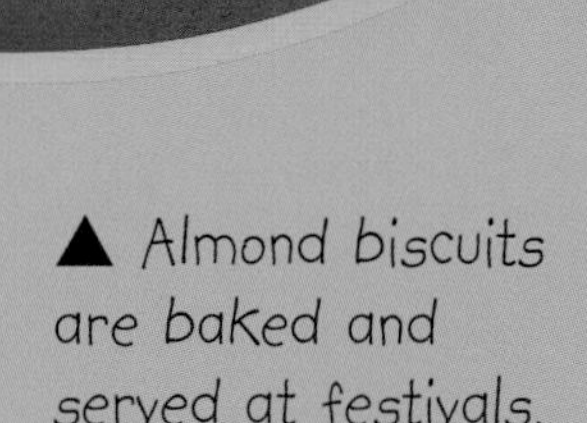

▲ Almond biscuits are baked and served at festivals.

Festival of Sacrifice

Eid-ul Adha (festival of sacrifice) is when Muslims remember the story of the prophet Ibrahim, who was asked by Allah to sacrifice his son, Is'mail (Ishmael), in order to show his love for Allah. At the last minute, Allah spared Is'mail and told Ibrahim to kill a sheep in his son's place.

Make some Eid party biscuits

You will need: 100g unsalted butter • 100g caster sugar • 200g flour • 20 blanched almonds • icing sugar • mixing bowl • wooden spoon • baking tray • sieve

1 Beat the butter and sugar in the bowl until light and fluffy. Mix in the flour with your hands until the mixture forms a dough. Add a little water, if needed.

2 Divide the dough into equal-sized small balls. Place an almond on top of each ball and flatten the balls with your fingers to form biscuit shapes.

3 Place the biscuits on a baking sheet and bake in the oven at 150°C (350°F) for 30 minutes. Let the biscuits cool, then sprinkle with icing sugar.

Family traditions

Important stages in a Muslim's life, such as birth, marriage and death, are marked by special religious traditions and ceremonies. Other traditions and customs are also observed in day-to-day life. Special rules guide Muslims as to what they are and are not allowed to do. Things that are allowed are called 'halal'. Things that are not allowed are called 'haram'.

Birth

After the birth of a child, the father whispers the shahadah (see page 6) in one of the baby's ears and the call to prayer in the other. He touches the baby's mouth with honey to sweeten it. It is traditional to name a baby seven days after the birth. The name chosen for a baby should have a good meaning. Baby boys are often named after one of the prophets. Girls may be named after one of the women in the prophet Muhammad's household, or one of the women mentioned in the Qur'an.

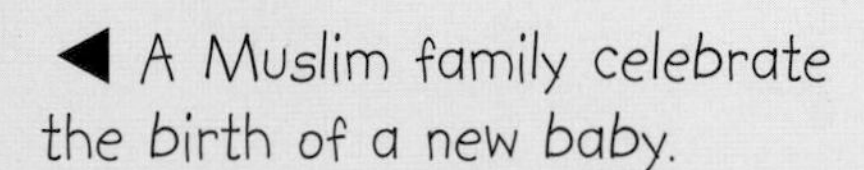

◀ A Muslim family celebrate the birth of a new baby.

Marriage

Islamic teaching encourages Muslims to marry and to start their own families. Marriage is seen as the joining of two families, not just two people, and parents often choose the marriage partner for their sons and daughters. Family and friends gather to celebrate the marriage and to give the newlyweds their blessing. There may be two wedding ceremonies: one at the signing of the marriage contract and the second when everyone gathers for a meal.

▲ A traditional Muslim wedding in Cairo, Egypt.

Death

After someone dies, the body is washed, wrapped in a simple cloth and then buried as soon as possible. At the funeral, family and friends gather and offer **Janazah**, which are prayers for the forgiveness of the person who has died. The body is buried with the face turned towards Makkah.

▶ These Muslim children are snacking on some dates.

Food

All types of food are halal (allowed) for Muslims except pork and alcohol. Dates and milk are popular ingredients in many dishes and are often eaten to break a fast. These two foods are always offered to guests as a welcome. The dates symbolize sweetness and the milk symbolizes purity.

The Hajj

Hajj, or the pilgrimage to Makkah, is the fifth pillar, when a Muslim shows devotion to God as part of a group. It takes place over a few days during the second week of Dhul Hijjah, the last month of the Islamic calendar. Every Muslim adult who can afford to must perform Hajj at least once in their life – if they are physically able. Parents often take children along, to introduce them to one of the most important rites in Islam. With pilgrims of all races and nationalities going for Hajj every year, it is the world's largest annual gathering.

▲ These pilgrims are dressing in their white clothes at the start of the Hajj.

The simple life

In Hajj, Muslims celebrate the story of God's guidance sent to humankind, starting with Adam and ending with Muhammad. Because it is a spiritual act, pilgrims must lead a simple life while performing it. Men wear two pieces of white seamless cloth. Women can wear any simple garment. This is to show that the pilgrims are not concerned with their clothing or other material things. It is also a sign of equality between all people. There is no distinction between people of different race or wealth in the eyes of God.

The Hajj begins

The first and most important act of Hajj is to walk around the Ka'ba seven times as Adam and Ibrahim did. The pilgrims also walk seven times between two nearby hills known as al Safa and al Marwa. This is to remember how Ibrahim's wife, Hajar, went searching for water for her baby Is'mail at this spot in the desert, after her husband left them there.

▲ These Hajj pilgrims are climbing down the Jebel al-Noor, or Mountain of Light, outside Makkah.

▲ Pilgrims on the plain of Arafat.

The end of the Hajj

The pilgrims ask for God's forgiveness on the plain of Arafat, where it is said that Adam and Eve were reunited after God forgave them. Later, they throw pebbles at the spot where they believe Satan tried to persuade Ibrahim not to obey God. In doing so, they declare their rejection of any temptations they might face in life. They also offer a sacrifice (as Ibrahim did). This act is done by all Muslim households, so that those not on the Hajj can share its spiritual message. This act marks the beginning of Eid-ul Adha. The last rite is to walk around the Ka'ba again – the farewell visit.

The spread of Islam

After the death of the prophet Muhammad, Islam spread rapidly across Asia, Africa and Europe. The early Muslims came from the deserts of Arabia, but they soon learned to adapt to new environments and mix with people of different traditions and cultures. Today, there are one billion Muslims worldwide.

Islam in Africa and Europe

Muslim merchants spread their faith to North Africa, where it remained close to the trade routes. From there, Muslims moved into Spain and established an Islamic civilization which lasted for 700 years. Many Spanish cities had magnificent Muslim palaces and impressive mosques. Today, about one million Muslim people live throughout Spain.

▼ Inside the Mezquita mosque in Cordoba, Spain.

China and Southeast Asia

Arab traders reached China, where a group gained the permission of the Chinese emperor to settle in his land. Today, there are around 200 million Muslims in China. Muslim merchants and traders were also the reason why Islam reached countries in Southeast Asia, including present-day Brunei, Malaysia and Indonesia. Indonesia now has the largest Muslim population in the world.

▲ Chinese Muslims looking at a Qur'an.

▼ Indonesian children attend Friday prayers at a mosque in Jakata.

Knowledge seekers

To seek knowledge is a good act in Islam, so Muslim scholars travelled in order to learn and to see the world. They usually travelled with trade **caravans** that crossed new lands. Many of them settled in the countries they visited and established new communities of Muslims. Others preferred to write about what they saw. Their writing provided those who didn't travel with information about life in these countries during those times. It was through the travelling of these seekers for knowledge that Islam came to be known and adopted as a religion by many people around the world.

Holy cities

Makkah, Madinah and **Jerusalem** are the three holiest cities in Islam. Each of these cities played an important part in Islamic history and contain some of Islam's holiest places. However, it is only to Makkah that every Muslim who is able makes a pilgrimage at least once in their lifetime.

Makkah

Makkah is the holiest city in Islam. Muslims believe that its sacred building, the Ka'ba, was originally built by the prophet Adam and then rebuilt by Ibrahim. It houses a black stone which Muslims believe the Angel Jibril gave to Ibrahim from heaven. In the past, it took pilgrims months to reach Makkah, either on foot or by camel. These days pilgrims arrive by aircraft in a matter of hours.

◀ The city of Makkah is in Saudi Arabia, in the Middle East.

The radiant city

Madinah is the second holiest city in Islam. Its name means 'the radiant city' because the arrival of Muhammad was thought to be a new spiritual beginning for the people who lived there. The mosque, which Muhammad helped to build, became the centre of the new community. Muhammad made Madinah his home and lived there until he died. Pilgrims often come to the city to visit the Prophet's Mosque after their journey to Makkah.

▲ The Prophet's Mosque in Madinah.

◀ The Dome of the Rock is built over the sacred rock. You can still see the rock inside the building.

Jerusalem

Jerusalem, in Israel, is the third holiest city in Islam. It is home to the third holiest mosque, the Al-Aqsa, and also to The Dome of the Rock. This is the place where Muhammad led all the prophets and messengers in prayer. Muslims believe that it was from here that Muhammad was lifted up to heaven, where God told him that Muslims must pray five times a day.

Al-Aqsa Mosque

The Al-Aqsa mosque is near the Dome of the Rock, in Haram al-Sharif, or the Noble Sanctuary – a complex of buildings, gardens and fountains. The name 'Al-Aqsa' means 'farthest mosque'. It was to the Al-Aqsa mosque that Muhammad came from Makkah on the night he visited the sacred rock.

Art and craft

Almost everything in a Muslim home or building, including the building itself, is an example of Muslim art. Muslims believe in making their lives perfect for Allah. By making everyday items such as rugs, books and fabrics beautiful, Muslim people believe they are showing their devotion to Allah. Most Islamic art features patterns made from shapes, flowers or Arabic calligraphy. This is because pictures of people or animals are not allowed, especially in places of worship.

Beautiful buildings

The Dome of the Rock and the Al-Aqsa mosque in Jerusalem, as well as the Taj Mahal in India, are examples of impressive Islamic buildings. Many Muslim buildings, including homes and many mosques, have flowing fountains at the centre of beautiful gardens.

▼ *The Taj Mahal was built by the Muslim emperor Shah Jahan as a tomb for his wife.*

Carpet and rug making

Muslim craftspeople are very talented at making carpets and rugs. Carpets made in Iran, Afghanistan and Turkey are some of the finest made anywhere in the world. Carpet makers compete among themselves to make the most stunning and complicated designs.

◀ Many carpets have very detailed designs in bright colours.

Calligraphy

Some Muslim artists specialize in the art of calligraphy. There are many different styles of calligraphy. In the past, it was done by hand with great care. Nowadays, artists may also use computers to create impressive calligraphy.

Make a decorated tile

You will need: 15cm x 15cm thick card • pencil • craft knife • masking tape • sponge • oil-based ceramic paint • 15cm x 15cm white tile • felt

1 Draw a design onto the cardboard. Ask an adult to carefully cut around the lines with a craft knife to make a stencil.

2 Tape the edges of the stencil to the tile with masking tape. Dab paint onto the tile through the stencil holes using a sponge.

3 Carefully remove the stencil and let the paint dry. Cut out a square of felt and glue it onto the back of your tile.

Activity

Make a model of the London Central Mosque

▲ The London Central Mosque is one of the best-known mosques in Britain. Its large golden dome can be seen from far away.

You will need: Two cereal boxes • scissors or a craft knife • glue • piece of red felt about 50cm x 25cm • black felt-tip • 50cm x 50cm square of thick white card • ruler • pencil • large sheets of white paper • a rounded yoghurt pot • gold paper (or gold paint or spray paint) • thin cardboard tube from the centre of a kitchen roll • sticky tack • sticky tape • two cocktail sticks

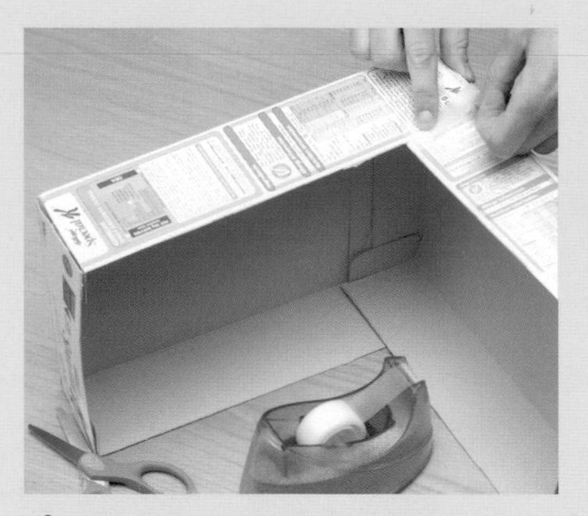

1 Cut the backs off the cereal boxes. Tape the boxes together to form an L-shape. This is the basis for the mosque.

2 Place the L-shape onto a piece of red felt. Draw around it with a black felt-tip pen and cut out. Glue the felt to the piece of white card.

3 Use a ruler and pencil to draw faint lines to divide up the other half of the card into squares, to look like a tiled courtyard.

4 Cover the L-shaped mosque in white paper. Glue the paper to the cereal boxes, to make the outside of the building look neat and tidy.

5 Draw arch shapes, each about 2cm wide, along the inside of the L-shape. Cut them out to make holes for the windows.

6 For the mosque's dome, cover the yoghurt pot with gold paper, or paint or spray it gold. (Ask an adult to help!)

7 Ask an adult to use scissors to cut away the rim of the yoghurt pot. Glue or tape the finished dome onto the top of your mosque.

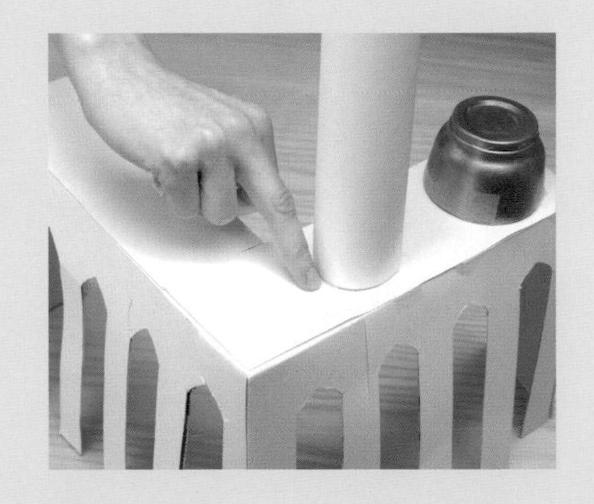

8 For the minaret, cover the cardboard tube with white paper, including the ends. Use sticky tack or tape to fix the tube to the roof, next to the dome.

9 Cut two small card crescent shapes (about 3cm tall) from cardboard and cover them in gold paper or spray them gold. Stick one end of a cocktail stick to the back of each crescent with tape.

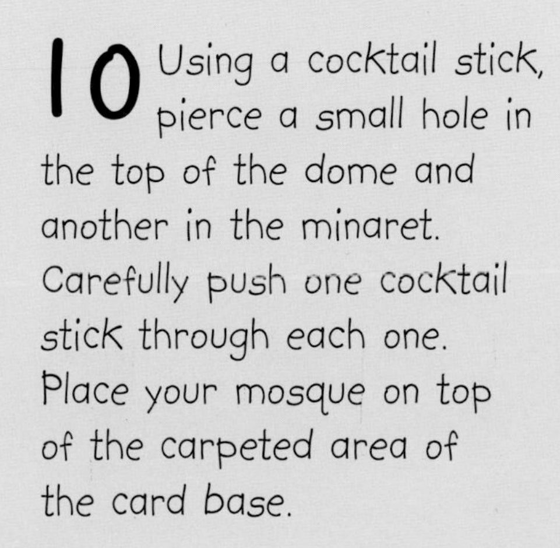

10 Using a cocktail stick, pierce a small hole in the top of the dome and another in the minaret. Carefully push one cocktail stick through each one. Place your mosque on top of the carpeted area of the card base.

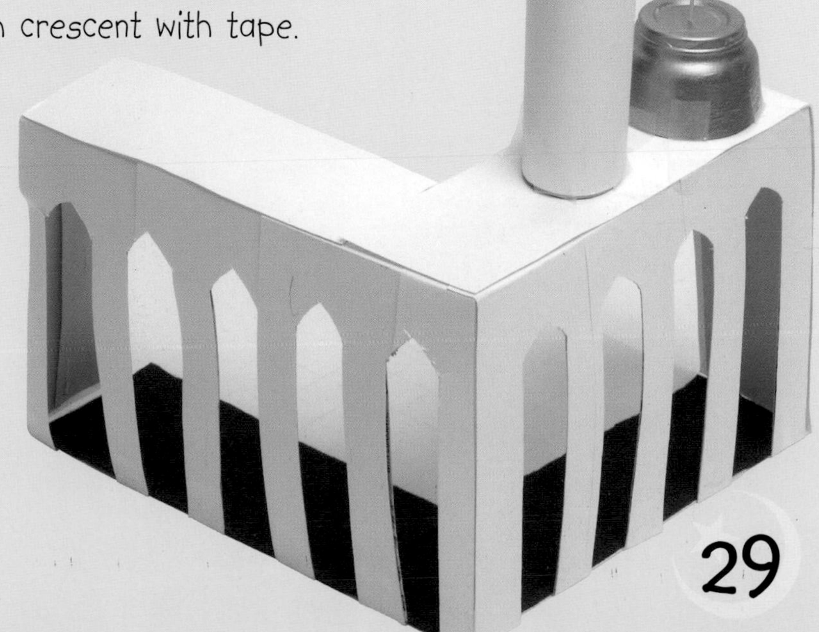

Glossary

Allah The Arabic word for God.

Arabic The language spoken in Arab countries such as Egypt, Iraq, Saudi Arabia and Morocco. Muslims believe that the angel Jibril spoke in Arabic when he told Allah's message to Muhammad.

calligraphy Beautiful handwriting. It is thought of as a type of art. People who write calligraphy as their job are called 'calligraphers'.

caravan A group of traders or other travellers journeying together.

fast A fast is a period of time during which you do not eat any food.

idol A statue or picture worshipped as a god.

Imam A Muslim teacher, or leader of the Muslim prayer.

Janazah Prayers for the forgiveness of the dead.

Jerusalem A city in Israel. It is the third most holy city in Islam and is home to the Al-Aqsa mosque and The Dome of the Rock.

Ka'ba The first place built for the worship of Allah. Muslims face it when they pray.

Madinah Madinah is a city in Saudi Arabia. It is the second most holy Muslim city. It is where Muhammad migrated to from Makkah, and where he helped to build the Prophet's Mosque.

Makkah A city in present day Saudi Arabia, where the ka'ba is found, and where Muhammad was visited many times by the angel Jibril. It is the most holy Muslim city.

meditate To think or reflect in a calm manner.

migrated To journey from one place or country to live in another.

mihrab An alcove in the wall of the mosque which the worshippers should face. It indicates the direction of the city of Makkah.

minaret A tower on a mosque. Traditionally used for calling Muslims to prayer.

mosque A building or place where Muslims worship and study together.

pilgrimage A special journey to a place of religious importance. People go on pilgrimages to show their devotion to god. People who are on a pilgrimage are called pilgrims.

prophet A person who receives a message from God and spreads the message on Earth.

Ramadan The ninth month of the Muslim calendar. Muslims fast during daylight hours of Ramadan.

recite To repeat aloud from memory.

Index

Notes for parents and teachers

Religions guidelines

This book is an accessible introduction to the beliefs and practices of the Muslim faith. It does not aim to be a comprehensive guide but gives plenty of opportunity for further activities and study. The content is closely linked to the non-statutory framework for Religious Education, particularly the QCA schemes of work listed below. The topics selected also overlap with locally agreed RE syllabuses.

Unit 1A: What does it mean to belong?
Unit 1D: Beliefs and practice
Unit 2C: Celebrations
Unit 2D: Visiting a place of worship
Unit 3A: What do signs and symbols mean in religion?
Unit 4D: What religions are represented in our neighbourhood?
Unit 5A: Why is Muhammad important to Muslims?
Unit 5B: How do Muslims express their beliefs through practices?
Unit 6B: Worship and community: what is the role of the mosque?
Unit 6C: Why are sacred texts important?
Unit 6D: What is the Qur'an and why is it important to Muslims?

List of some useful websites:

Islamic Awareness Week: http://www.iaw.org.uk
Islamic Relief: http://www.islamic-relief.com
Muslim Aid: http://www.muslimaid.org
Muslim Heritage www.muslimheritage.com
The Virtual Classroom
www.isb.org.uk/virtual/newsite

For educational resources, artefacts and children's literature contact:

The Islamic Foundation: www.islamic-foundation.org.uk
The Muslim Educational Trust: www.muslim-ed-trust.org.uk
Discover Islam: www.discoverislam.com

To arrange for group/school visits or to find out about how mosques work contact:

The East London Mosque:
http://www.eastlondonmosque.org.uk
The Muslim Cultural Heritage Centre (Al Manar):
http://www.mchc.org.uk

Projects for the children to try

- Create an Eid postcard for an imaginary pen-friend in Australia and write a message on the back describing what you saw and how how you felt when you visited a mosque with your school.
- Make a list of names of your Muslim friends. Find out about their meanings in English and in your friends' own language(s).
- Invite your friends to an Eid party and serve them almond Eid biscuits.

For the activity on page 13, the following websites show the alphabet in Arabic and English:
http://pistolero.unilang.org/arabe/index.html
www.blss.portsmouth.sch.uk